# *William Bolcom*

# Housemusic

*for flute and piano*

ISBN 978-1-4950-6309-1

www.ebmarks.com
www.halleonard.com

*for Penny and Martha Fischer*

# HOUSEMUSIC

WILLIAM BOLCOM
(2014)

## 1. Hustle and Bustle

NB: Accidentals obtain throughout a beamed group and, as a courtesy, are repeated within measures for ease of reading.

15
tr
fzp
mf
fast rolls
19
(tr)
mf
p
p
23
3
fast rolls
mf
mf
p
27
p
cresc.
fz
f
p
cresc.
fz
f

31
mp
mp
cresc.
cresc.
35
ff
ff
8
tr
mp
mp
39
tr
43
tratt.
a tempo
dim.
dim.
p
p

47
3
f
mp
52
dim.
pp
July 9, 2014
Ann Arbor

# 2. Like an Old Song

*William Bolcom*

# Housemusic

*for flute and piano*

ISBN 978-1-4950-6309-1

www.ebmarks.com
www.halleonard.com

Flute

*for Penny and Martha Fischer*

# HOUSEMUSIC

WILLIAM BOLCOM
(2014)

## 1. Hustle and Bustle

NB: Accidentals obtain throughout a beamed group and, as a courtesy, are repeated within measures for ease of reading.

27
p
cresc.
fz
f
31
mp
cresc.
35
ff
38
mp
tratt.
a tempo
43
dim.
p
47
f
51
mp
dim.
pp

# 2. Like an Old Song

tratt. a tempo
24
mp
f
p
30
34
cresc. poco
mf
dim.
38
p
mp
42

# 3. Rigaudon

Joyous ♩. = 69
Pno.
5
p
f
mf
9
cresc.
12
f
mf
fz
17
tr
mp
cresc.
f
espr.
dim.
p
22
mp
f
mp

27
tr
fz
p
Pno.
32
mp
cresc.
37
f
cresc.
ff
41
cresc.
fff
44
dim.
mp
dim.
48
poco a poco
pp
1
p

16
p
pp
p
cresc.
cresc.
19
tratt.
a tempo
f
dim.
p
f
dim.
mp
23
tratt.
mp
f
cresc.
mf
dim.
26
a tempo
p
simile
p

July 10, 2014
Ann Arbor

# 3. Rigaudon

16
fz
mp
cresc.
f
espr.
dim.
p
p
cresc.
f
p
21
mp
f
mp
mf
p
26
fz
p
pp
mf
dim.
pp
p
31
mp
mp
p

July 12, 2014
Ann Arbor